How to Make Perfect
Dollhouse Figures

Kitty Mackey

KALMBACH
BOOKS

To Terry:
Still two playful otters in the beaver pond of life

Printed in the United States of America

98 99 00 01 02 03 04 05 06 07 08   10 9 8 7 6 5 4 3 2 1

For more information, visit our website at
http://www.kalmbach.com

Publisher's Cataloging in Publication
(Provided by Quality Books, Inc.)

Mackey, Kitty.
   How to make perfect dollhouse figures / Kitty Mackey. —
1st ed.
   48 p.   215 x 279 cm.
   ISBN: 0-89024-341-7

   1. Dollmaking. 2. Cloth dolls—Design and construction.
3. Polymer clay craft.   I. Title.

TT175.M33 1998   745.592'21
                             QBI97-41479

Book and cover design: Kristi Ludwig

Cover photo: Alice Korach
All photos and illustrations are by the author, unless otherwise noted.

Contents

Introduction

Me? Sculpt a doll?

Yes, you can! You can learn to sculpt your own realistic 1-inch scale figures. Whether you call them dolls or figures, sculptures or figurines, this book will teach you the skills you need to make your own little personalities for miniature scenes or displays.

Don't worry about being "all thumbs" or "unable to draw a straight line"! Figure sculpting doesn't require a single straight line and you'll be using simple hand tools—not your thumbs.

You can learn to recognize facial features and body proportions! Although you see faces every day, once you start to sculpt you'll begin to really look at faces and study facial features. You'll also learn how to analyze the body in terms of basic geometric shapes.

You can find the patience! Patience is really just time put to good use. If you take the time—even just a few minutes each day—to work on your sculpting, you will eventually see results from your efforts.

No more excuses! You *can* learn how to make miniature figures! All you really need is to enjoy what you're doing. Once you get started, you'll gain confidence in what you can do.

And that confidence starts with this, your first figure, so don't be intimidated by the idea of perfection. In fact, forget perfection—it's a dangerous preoccupation that prevents us from trying new things. Just have fun watching the miniature personalities emerge (as they will!) from a ball of clay and your own hands.

The techniques in this book begin with a wire armature bent into a simple stick figure. Once the armature is complete, you simply add shaped pieces of clay to the armature until you achieve the final figure. It's that easy.

Instructions are provided for two kinds of figures. One figure is sculpted entirely from clay—clothes and all. The other figure has clay head, hands, and feet, but the armature is wrapped in cloth and the clothes are sewn. Both figures demonstrate different features that provide you with a variety of techniques. Choose whichever method you like, or change them to meet the needs of your figure's personality. The decision is entirely yours.

So, can you sculpt your own figures? Yes, you can!

1
Equip Your Studio

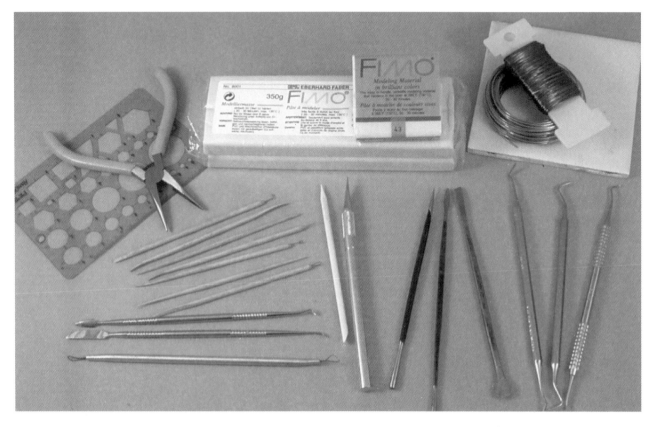

Both basic and optional tools and supplies are shown in this photo. Clockwise from top: Fimo, 26- and 18-gauge wire on a 4-inch ceramic tile, three dental tools; three wax-sculpting tools, X-Acto knife, cuticle stick, wire scooping tool, kit modeling tools from Squadron Products, micro-modeling tools from Perfect Touch, circle template, needle-nose pliers.

Sculpting and Modeling Tools

An ordinary cuticle stick is a useful, all-purpose sculpting tool. To make the cuticle stick even more useful, alter the rounded end of the cuticle stick as shown in Diagram 1-1. Many other everyday items, such as yarn needles, crochet hooks, and toothpicks are also useful for shaping small areas of clay. The following list, however, contains many types of tools that are designed specifically for finely detailed work.

• Dental probes, files, and excavators are useful for sculpting facial features and other fine details.
• Wax-sculpting tools are made from hand-forged steel and are available in a variety of shapes and sizes. Because the tools are strong they are especially useful for pushing or smoothing out large areas of clay. Although some wax-sculpting tools are too large for use with 1-inch scale figures, most sets include two or three tools, such as those shown in the photo, that are invaluable.

• Clay wires designed for use with wheel-thrown pottery are useful for scooping out small areas of clay when making folds and creases in clothing.
• Various types of metal-sculpting tools produced for model kit enthusiasts, such as tools available from Squadron Products, are also useful for clay sculpting.
• Micro-modeling tools are available in many sizes and shapes (in addition to the selection shown in the photo). Use these delicate hand-finished tools to add fine details to small areas.

5

Tools, Materials, and Supplies

- Ceramic tiles, nonglare white, large (8″) and small (4″)
- Circle template
- Cuticle stick, wooden (also called orangewood stick)
- Denatured alcohol
- Fimo: Flesh color, no. 43
- Paintbrushes, sable, 5/0 or smaller liners; assorted sizes and shapes, such as ¼″ flat, beveled, filbert, and round
- Premoistened wipes
- Needle-nose pliers
- Oven thermometer
- Paints and paint supplies: acrylics, oils (as noted in text)
- Sculpting and modeling tools (as noted in text)
- Window cleaner, clear
- Wire, unpainted, 26 and 18 gauge (28 and 19 gauge are also suitable)
- Wire cutters
- X-Acto knife and sharp blades

Optional Tools, Materials and Supplies

- Soft pastels (artist's chalks)
- Color wheel
- Creative Paperclay
- Fimo Mix-Quick or Transparent no. 01
- Fimo: Terra-cotta (no. 77); Ochre (no. 17)
- Pasta machine

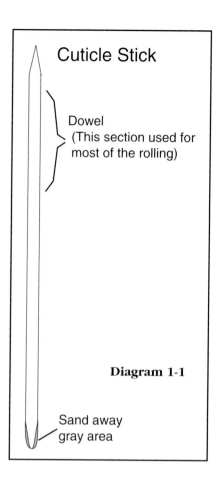

Cuticle Stick

Dowel
(This section used for most of the rolling)

Sand away gray area

Diagram 1-1

SOURCES

Dental tools. Check the yellow pages for dental supply companies.

Perfect Touch, 24 Artesia, Conroe TX 77304 (micro-modeling tools)

Squadron Products, 1115 Crowley Drive, Carrollton, TX 75011-5010 (tools and supplies for hobbyists)

Jerry's Artarama Inc., P. O. Box 58638, Raleigh, NC 27658; 1-800-U-ARTIST (art supplies, including polymer clay and wax-sculpting tools)

Micro-Mark: The Small Tool Specialists, 340 Snyder Ave., Berkeley Heights, NJ 07922-1595; 1-800-225-1066 (paints, tools, and supplies for hobbyists)

The Clay Factory, P. O. Box 460598, Escondido, CA 92046-0598; 1-800-243-3466 (polymer clay and related supplies)

2
Work with Polymer Clay

Polymer-based clays are sold under several brand names, including Fimo, Puppen (Doll) Fimo, Cernit, Premo Sculpey, Sculpey III, and Friendly Clay.

The instructions in this book refer specifically to Fimo. Fimo is pliable enough to shape easily, yet stiff enough to hold fine details. Flesh-colored Fimo also produces a realistic light flesh-colored skin tone after baking, an important consideration, since the skin areas will not be painted.

The choice of which brand of clay to use often comes down to personal preference. Because clay is affected by the warmth of the hands and ambient temperature, different people experience slightly different results from the same type of clay. Also, companies change formulas, so the properties of the clays may vary—a clay that was too soft last year may be just right this year. You may want to experiment with different types of clay, or mix brands together for a color and texture you like.

Like many polymer clays, Fimo can get old and can even partially cure if not properly stored, so always test the freshness of the clay before beginning a project. To test, open the package, cut the block into eight or ten pieces and roll one piece on a clean work surface. If it crumbles and feels dry—don't use it. The clay is either too old or has been partially cured by excessive heat. If it breaks into three or four pieces, pick them up, roll them in your hands for a few minutes, and roll the piece out again. If the clay holds together and feels moist, continue to roll it in your hands and on the surface a few more times. If after a few minutes you are able to form the clay into a smooth ball, it is fresh. Prepare all the clay by rolling small pieces into smooth balls.

If after preparing the clay you find that it is too stiff, mix Fimo Mix-Quick or Transparent Fimo into the flesh-colored clay. Use equal proportions of Mix-Quick in all the clay and never add more than one part Mix-Quick to eight parts flesh-colored clay. Mixing the Mix-Quick or transparent clay into the flesh-colored clay also gives it the quality of lovely, translucent porcelain.

You may choose to use a pasta machine to soften or roll out large quantities of clay. If so, be aware that even after extensive use and cleaning, the stainless steel rollers may leave gray-colored metallic residue on the clay. To avoid contaminating the clay, use the machine to roll only clay that will be used in areas that will be painted. The pasta machine is very useful, however, for rolling out flat pieces of clay for clothes and accessories.

Because the flesh areas of the doll will not be painted, keep your work space clean. Start by cleaning the ceramic tiles, which you will use as a work surface, with clear window cleaner. As you work, clean your hands frequently with premoistened wipes. Use good grease-cutting dish soap to remove built-up clay from your hands and work surface, followed by a final rinsing with clear water to remove any soapy residue. If you find that your hands dry out too much from the clay, use conditioning hand cream at the end of each session.

If the clay becomes too soft as you work (from the warmth of your hands and work lights) let the project sit for a few hours or overnight.

Baking Fimo

Polymer clay emits a funny smell when baked, so always work with adequate ventilation, both during and after baking. Oven temperature is a critical element—the oven must be hot enough to cure the clay completely, but not so hot that the clay burns and discolors. Use an oven thermometer to achieve accurate, consistent results and perform the following tests before baking the finished project.

To start the baking test, heat the oven to 245 degrees Fahrenheit, place a ¾-inch ball of softened clay on a ceramic tile in the center of the oven, and bake for one hour. Do not open the oven door during baking; let the piece cool completely before removing it from the oven. If the clay ball feels soft and you can easily gouge it with a fingernail, the oven was too cool. If the clay turned a yellowish color, the oven was too hot. Adjust the temperature as needed—and possibly the baking time, but never bake the piece for less than 30 minutes. Continue to bake test pieces until the test ball feels hard and crisp, has the right color, and can't be easily gouged. Even after proper curing, polymer clay can be carved and sanded, so don't expect the piece to be as hard as glass or as durable as metal.

Polymer clay projects can also be baked in stages, if desired. The instructions in this book show how to finish the figure completely before baking, but if you choose to build your figure in stages, keep these points in mind:
• The clay has a tendency to darken if baked too often.
• The joint between raw clay and baked clay will not be as strong as a single piece with no joint.
• Lines where unbaked clay is added to baked clay are nearly impossible to hide. Try to make areas that will not be painted—such as the face and hands—all at once.

Fixing Defects

If you bake the clay at the appropriate temperature and allow it to cool slowly, it should not develop any defects. Two problems that may occur are bubbling and cracking. Don't assume, however, that a defect must be fixed before you explore creative ways of incorporating the defect into the figure—often, defects lead to good effects!

Bubbling may result if the temperature of the oven is too high or if the figure is placed too close to the heating elements. If the clay bubbles or blisters in an area that will be painted, simply sand off the defective area and patch with air-hardening clay such as Creative Paperclay. If bubbles are on the face, hands, or other areas of the body that will not be painted, look for a creative way to hide the defect— put gloves on bubbled hands, or wrap a bandage around a defective knee, for example. If that won't work, remove the section and sculpt it over.

The clay may crack for a number of reasons: the oven is too hot; the piece is cooled too quickly; the clay was not well conditioned. Built-up gases locked inside the figure may also cause cracking. As you sculpt, clay has a tendency to pull away from the armature—especially the head—leaving a hollow space. The gases produced when the clay is heated may build up in hollows until they break through at the weakest spot— typically the neck. To avoid this problem, use a large needle to make a small hole in the back of the neck, just under the hairline, preferably in an area that will be painted. Poke the hole all the way to the armature. The hole will vent the gases and help prevent major cracks. After the figure is baked and cooled, fill the hole with a small piece of air-hardening clay such as Creative Paperclay and paint.

Small hairline cracks may also appear on the surface after the figure is baked. These cracks are usually caused by insufficient blending as pieces of clay are added to the figure. To avoid this problem, smooth all the surfaces with denatured alcohol applied with a fine sable paintbrush. Denatured alcohol is a solvent for polymer clay—so use it very sparingly and practice on a large part of the figure that will be painted before working on the facial features.

Mixing Skin Tones

It's easy to make different types of skin simply by adding colored clay to softened Fimo or, in the case of African-American skin color, by painting the baked Fimo. If you plan to mold the clothing onto the body, any parts of the figure that will not be covered with clothing should be tinted the preferred skin tone.
Tint the clay by adding color to clay that has been softened and rolled into balls as previously described. If you add too much color, just mix in more of the softened flesh color. Mix enough tinted clay all at once, as it's nearly impossible to match two tinted batches. To make an adult with face, neck, hands, and lower arms exposed, tint at least half of a 65-gram block of clay. Err on the side of more rather than less—you can always use any extra clay on clothing that will be painted. Of course, you may choose to tint the entire batch of clay.

The following list of formulas is by no means exhaustive. Each type of skin tone is unique and requires experimentation, but the formulas will help to get you started.

Caucasian: Often, the flesh-colored clay straight from the package is too light for the desired complexion. To make a ruddier complexion, add just a pinch of terra-cotta (no. 77) to the softened clay. Add more or less terra-cotta to get the desired color.

African-American: It's possible to achieve a pleasing skin color by mixing different colors of Fimo, but the resulting clay is too soft to hold details. You might also try using a different brand of clay, such as ProMat brown no. 2052. Another alternative is to paint the figure, in which case you must choose paint that will adhere well to Fimo without leaving brush strokes. Both Pactra acrylic enamel, flat light earth (no. A23), and Badger Model Flex dark Tuscan oxide red provide excellent coverage and coloring. You may wish to experiment with other types of paints.

American Indian: To the softened clay add very small pieces of terra-cotta, one at a time, until the desired complexion is achieved. You might also try adding a pinch of ochre (no. 17) to balance the reddish color.

Asian: To the conditioned clay, add very small pieces of ochre (no. 17) one at a time, until the desired complexion is achieved.

3
Paint the Figure

Painting Clothes and Hair

Because cured Fimo is nonporous, some acrylic and water-based paints do not adhere well to the baked clay. Oil paints and other solvent-based paints, on the other hand, can react negatively with the clay if used to cover large areas. Some manufacturers of polymer clay discourage the use of oil-based paints.

The following types of water-based acrylic paints, however, have been thoroughly tested and provide excellent coverage on polymer clay. Except where noted, for a day or so after painting acrylic paint is very easy to wash or peel off—so if you really don't like your paint job, just wash off the paint and start over. After a few days, the paint will cure and become more permanent. This list is by no means exhaustive; experi-

ment with different types of water-based paints to discover your own favorites.
• Acrylic bottled paints like Apple Barrel, Ceramcoat by Delta, Home Decor, Americana, Folk Art, and Accent. These are available in a wide variety of colors, most of which are opaque.
• Pactra Acrylic Enamels and Badger Model Flex acrylics. Because these paints were designed for airbrush work, the pigments are extremely fine. When applied with a paintbrush, the paints color the clay without masking the texture of the clay.
• Aero Colors by Schmincke. These brilliant, translucent colors adhere to Fimo and color without hiding details. For best adhesion on Fimo, wipe down the baked clay first with isopropyl alcohol and use the alcohol, rather than water, as a

medium and cleaner. Aero Colors stain Fimo on contact, so if you want to remove them, immediately use isopropyl alcohol. Take care to avoid spilling paint on skin areas of the figure that will be left unpainted.

To achieve the appearance of depth on clothing using opaque acrylics, apply at least three coats of paint, each a different color. Clothing painted with just one color is flat and lifeless; but clothes take on additional depth and life when painted with a dark undercoat, a main color, and a highlight color. Select the colors for the three layers as follows.

1. Choose the main color and darken it by mixing it with its complementary color (the opposite color on the color wheel). Apply a solid coat of the undercoat color and let dry; apply a second coat if necessary.

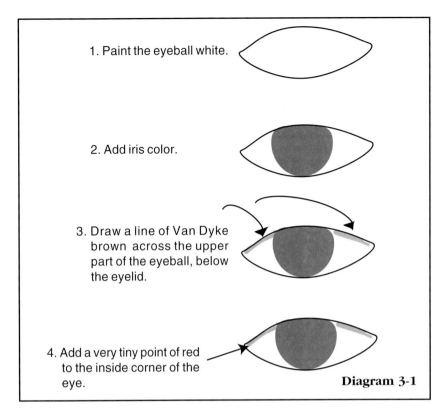

1. Paint the eyeball white.

2. Add iris color.

3. Draw a line of Van Dyke brown across the upper part of the eyeball, below the eyelid.

4. Add a very tiny point of red to the inside corner of the eye.

Diagram 3-1

2. Apply a layer of the main color, but leave the undercoat color showing through here and there—especially in the folds. Let dry.

3. For the highlights, either lighten the main color by adding a little white, or choose another color that is a shade lighter than the main color. Drybrush this color on the high points of the piece.

Do not use the three-layer system when painting with Schmincke Aero Colors. Instead, apply one or two coats of the desired finished color; allow the paint to puddle in folds and creases. The extra paint will dry darker and provide the illusion of depth.

Painting the Eyes and Lips

The rule of thumb for painting eyes and lips this small is: less is more! Guard against the temptation to paint in every eyelash and freckle!

You can use acrylic paints to paint the eyes and lips, but oil paints stay workable for a long time, which is useful when painting eyes. Since the area being covered is so small, the paints adhere well to the polymer clay and will not react negatively. Many oil paints and mediums, moreover, are available in synthetic formulas, which make them even better suited for use on polymer clay. Mix just a drop of linseed oil into oil paint to make the paint smooth and workable.

Use a very small liner brush (5/0 or smaller) to paint the eyes, following the steps in Diagram 3-1 and using the following suggested colors.

For brown eyes: white, Van Dyck brown, and cadmium red For blue eyes: white, Prussian blue, and cadmium red

Most lip colors start with a base color of cadmium red lightened with a little bit of white. Add more or less white to vary the shade of pink; add burnt sienna to darken the lips. To paint the lips, draw a thin line of paint across the center line of the lips. That simple line may be enough for closed-mouth lips.

However, if you want fuller lips, paint in the lobe of the lower lip and add a thicker line for the upper lip using a slightly darker shade of red.

Finally, if you want to add a touch of blush to the figure's cheeks, scrape a piece of red soft pastel with a piece of sandpaper. Use a very small paintbrush to pick up the red dust and brush it onto the cheeks. If the cheeks turn too red, just wipe off the color with a damp tissue and try again. (If you apply the blush before baking the figure, it will be more permanent—but it's not as easy to correct if you make a mistake.)

Metallic Effects

You can simulate the look of gold, silver, copper, and bronze on polymer clay with metal-foil leafing systems, such as Delta Renaissance Foil, and metallic powders, such as Friendly Metallic Powder. Metal foils are better for applications that call for a mottled effect; powders are better for accessories that require solid coverage.

To use the metal foil, roll out a sheet of colored clay in a pasta machine. Lay the foil, dull side down, on top of the rolled-out Fimo; roll the clay and foil through the pasta machine (with the machine on one setting lower than that used to roll the sheet of clay). From the metallic-mottled clay sheet, cut out special accessories such as purses, belts, hats, or even armor, shields, or swords and add them to the unbaked figure. To use the metallic powder on unbaked clay, simply brush the powder onto the clay with a soft paintbrush. If the clay is baked, mix the powder with a little clear acrylic gloss and paint it onto the clay. The powder-gloss mixture dries quickly, but the effect is better than that possible with many pre-mixed bottled metallic paints.

4
Learn the Terms & Techniques

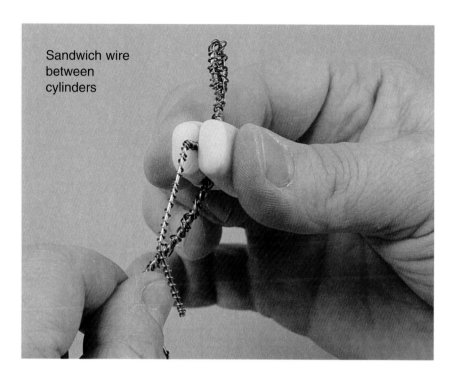

Sandwich wire between cylinders

Take a few minutes to familiarize yourself with these terms and techniques, which will be used throughout the book.

"Sandwich wire between cylinders"

This technique is the main method used to cover the wire armature. Place one cylinder of clay on each side of the wire and roll the seam smooth, as follows.

"Roll smooth" or "roll the seam smooth"

Holding the cuticle stick between thumb and fingertips, with the pointed end facing the clay, gently roll the cuticle stick back and forth over the clay until the seams created by joining pieces of the clay are blended. Use just a light amount of pressure on the cuticle stick while rolling. Use the pointed tip for small areas; use the dowel for large areas.

"Feather the edges"

Use the flat side of the cuticle stick to gently pull the edges of the added clay into the main mass of clay. Continue until all raw edges are blended.

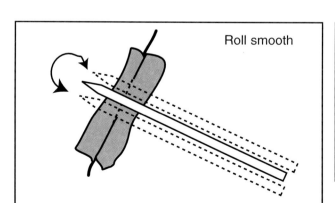

Roll smooth

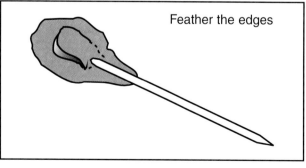

Feather the edges

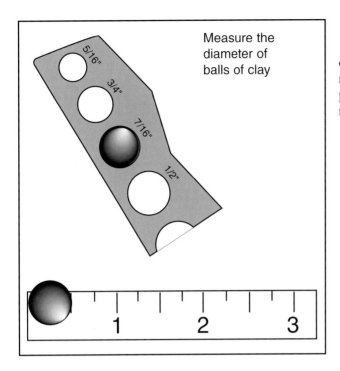

Measure the diameter of balls of clay

"Measure the diameter of balls of clay"

Using the diameter of a ball of clay provides a consistent method for adding clay to the figure. To measure the diameter, roll a ball of clay as round as possible and check the size by holding it up to a ruler or a circle template.

The following terms and familiar shapes are referred to throughout the text.

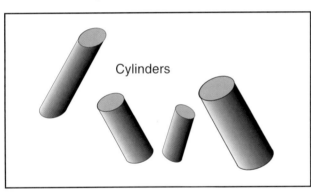

Cylinders

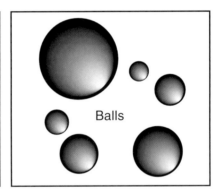

Balls

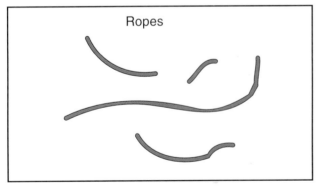

Ropes

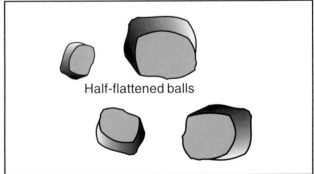

Half-flattened balls

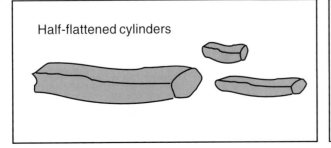

Half-flattened cylinders

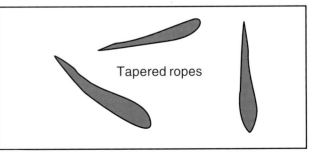

Tapered ropes

5
Learn Basic Principles of Anatomy

Proportion and Movement
Unless you plan to represent figures such as hobbits and elves (and even those figures follow consistent rules), your figures should follow two basic guidelines for realistic representations: proportion and movement.

Proportion refers simply to how the parts of the body fit with one another. The head should not be too large or too small; the arms should not hang down to the knees; the nose should not be so large that it overshadows the features of the face, and it should be on the same plane as the ears. The diagrams on the following pages provide basic principles of anatomy and proportion, most of which have been handed down from the artists of Classical Greece. Keep in mind that the

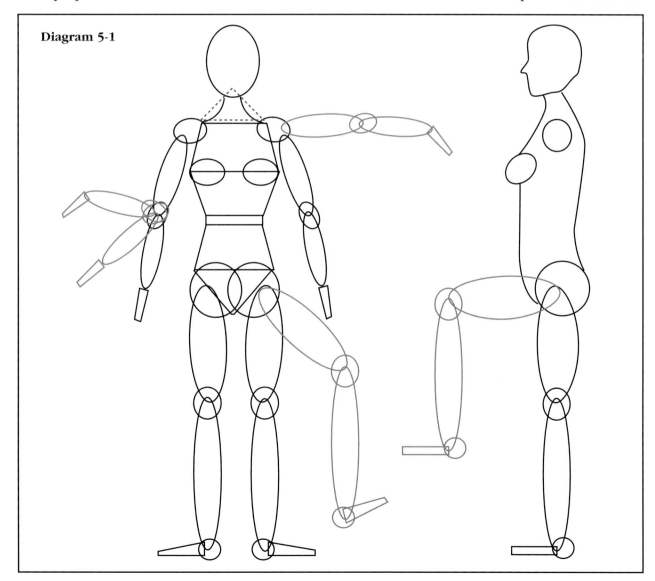

Diagram 5-1

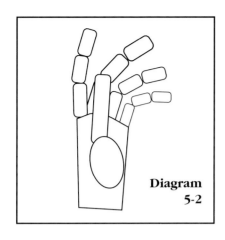

Diagram 5-2

proportions shown are not hard-and-fast rules—just general guidelines based on observations made by artists throughout the ages. There will be times, of course, when you will want to exaggerate features, such as eyes, for comic effect. Even so, the doll will still look realistic if the overall proportions are maintained and if the pose is believable.

The pose, or movement, of the body refers to basic mechanics of the body's joints. Knees only bend in one direction, for example, while the shoulder socket allows the arm to rotate 360 degrees. The mechanics of movement—and subsequent poses that are possible—provide one the best ways to make your sculpted figure convey a desired emotion. In other words, make an understanding of body language a part of your sculpting toolbox.

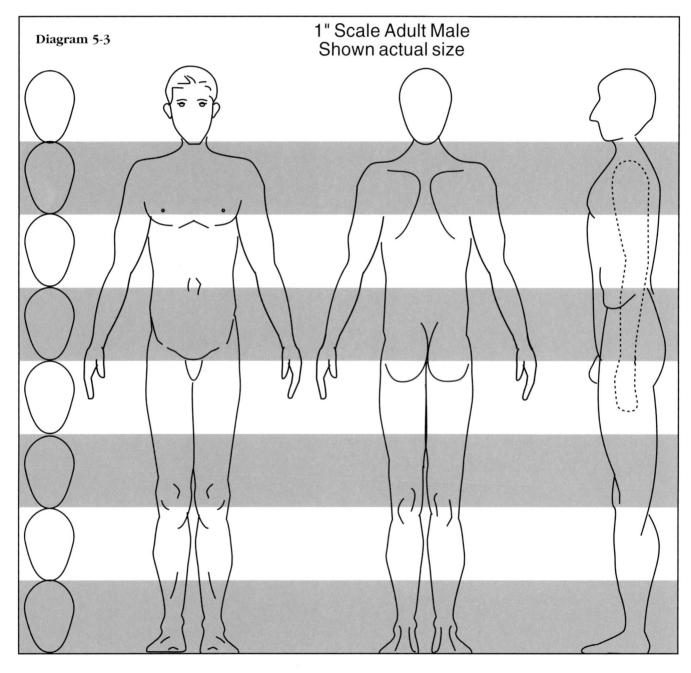

Diagram 5-3

1" Scale Adult Male
Shown actual size

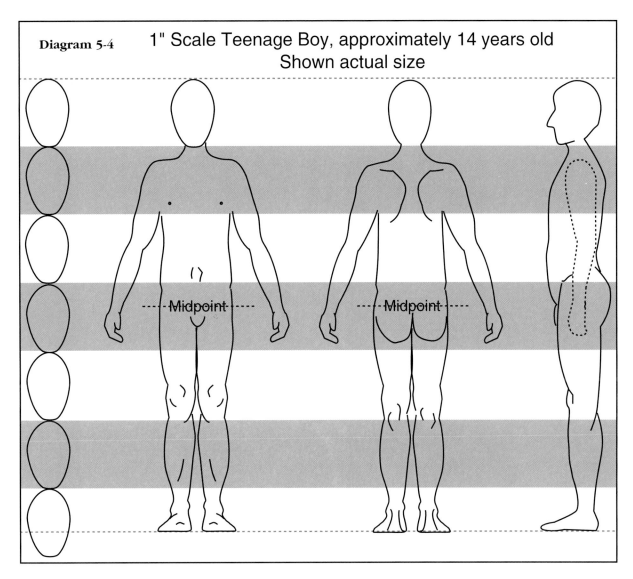

Diagram 5-4

1" Scale Teenage Boy, approximately 14 years old
Shown actual size

Midpoint

Midpoint

You can study body language anywhere there are people to watch. The next time you're standing in a long line at a store, observe the positions of people waiting in line. Look at the angry person. The full weight of the body is equally distributed on both feet—and the feet are probably on the same plane and a little more than shoulder distance apart. The arms are probably either crossed or jutted against the hips, and the head is most likely straight. Now look at the person catching up on the tabloid news. The weight of the body is probably shifted more to one side, giving the body a gentle S-shaped curve. One foot is probably a little ahead of the other.

The head may be tilted, and the arms relaxed. People cheering at a football game rarely have their arms hanging limp at their sides; sleepy people have a rounded back and rounded joints.

As you make casual observations and study the human body, you will soon notice that the body is basically a collection of geometric shapes, as demonstrated in Diagrams 5-1 and 5-2. Even the hand—perhaps the most efficient machine of all—is less intimidating to artists and sculptors when viewed as a collection of simple geometric shapes.

The idealized drawings in Diagrams 5-3 through 5-9 represent front, side, and back views of male and female bodies at dif-

ferent ages. These drawings are shown full size for "average" figures in 1-inch scale. (In 1-inch scale, one inch is equal to one foot, so the 6-inch high drawing of the male would be the equivalent of a 6-foot-tall full-size man.)

Notice that these representations use the head, rather than fractional inches, as a unit of measurement. Head-height is a commonly used guideline that allows for variations in height and stature while still maintaining proportions. The diagram shows adult figures that are each eight head-heights tall. In reality, 7½ head-heights is a more accurate measurement, but many artists use eight head-heights simply for ease of measurement.

Keep in mind that all the drawings are idealized and do not take into account individual differences. Such differences are for you—the artist—to see and incorporate into your figures. Refer to the drawings as you sculpt to help maintain accurate proportions, but deviate from the idealized types when necessary.

You may find it useful to make a template of the idealized body types to have close at hand while you're working. To make a simple template, copy or trace the desired illustration, glue the copy onto heavy cardboard, and cut out the shape. The resulting "paper doll" will save a lot of flipping pages back and forth.

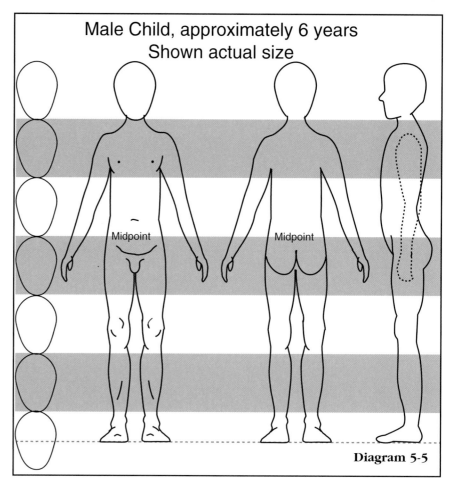

Male Child, approximately 6 years
Shown actual size

Diagram 5-5

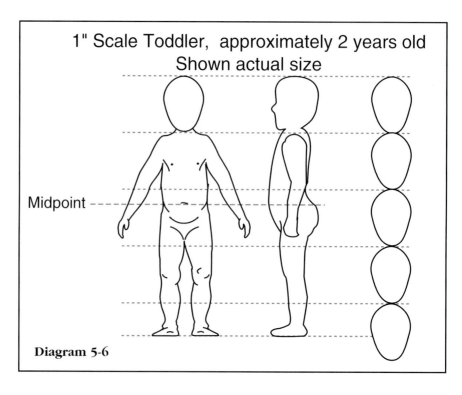

1" Scale Toddler, approximately 2 years old
Shown actual size

Diagram 5-6

16

Diagram 5-7

1" Scale Adult Female
Shown actual size

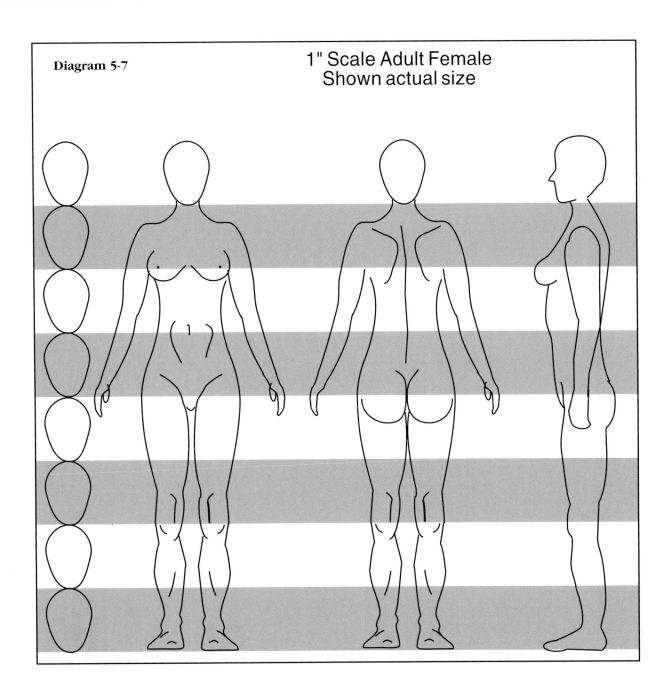

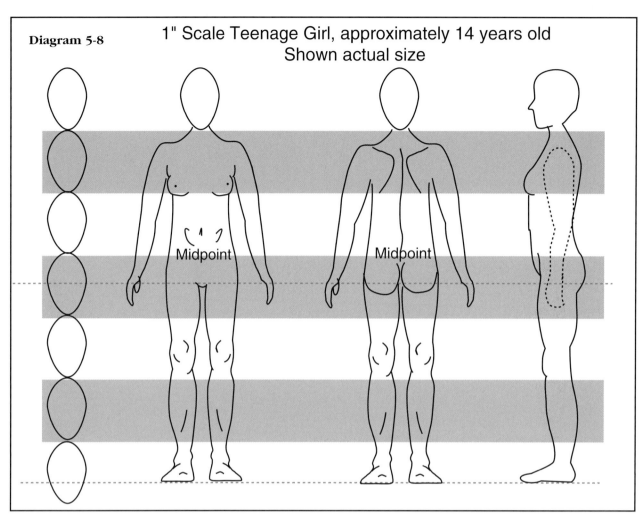

Diagram 5-8

1" Scale Teenage Girl, approximately 14 years old
Shown actual size

Midpoint

Midpoint

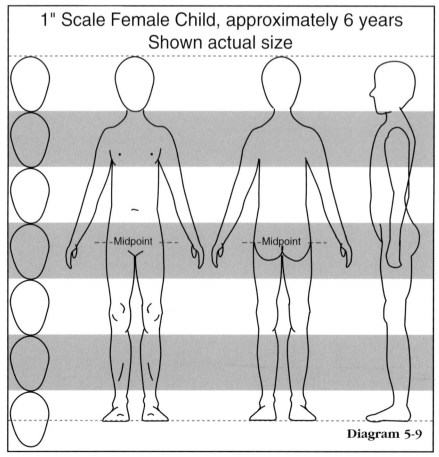

1" Scale Female Child, approximately 6 years
Shown actual size

Midpoint

Midpoint

Diagram 5-9

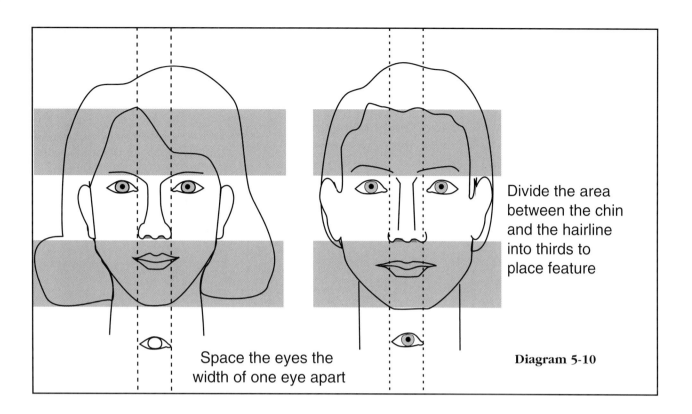

Divide the area between the chin and the hairline into thirds to place feature

Space the eyes the width of one eye apart

Diagram 5-10

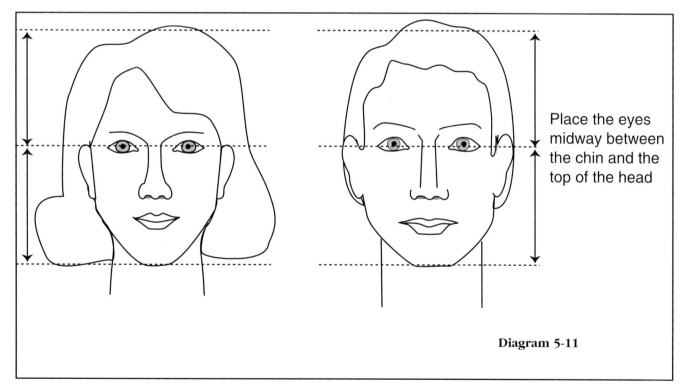

Place the eyes midway between the chin and the top of the head

Diagram 5-11

Proportions of the Face

Nature was kind to sculptors when she designed the proportions of the head and facial features. The brow, nose, and lips are easy to place when the face is divided into three equal sections between the chin and hairline, as shown in Diagram 5-10. When the head is divided into two equal sections between the chin and the crown, the eyes fall right in the center (Diagram 5-11). You can even use the face to make sure the hands aren't too large or too small, as shown in Diagram 5-12: with the heel of the hand placed on the chin, the fingers should rest just below the hairline. (Try it—it works almost every time!)

19

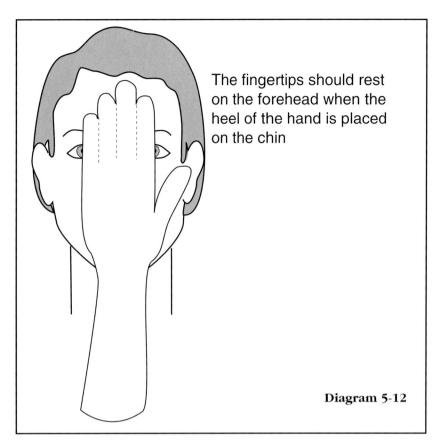

The fingertips should rest on the forehead when the heel of the hand is placed on the chin

Diagram 5-12

Viewed in profile, the distance from the end of the nose to the front of the ear is equal to the distance from the brow line to the chin, as shown by the gray square in Diagram 5-13. The close-up profile in Diagram 5-14 demonstrates the planes that define the relationship among nose, lips, chin, and forehead. In figures as small as 1-inch scale, such differences are subtle, but no less deserving of attention than in a larger figure. You'll find that often just one small piece of clay, properly placed, will add sparkle to an otherwise lifeless face.

The idealized drawings provided are essential for reference, but you'll still need to use a model—in most cases a photograph is sufficient. Even if you don't want your figure to look like any particular person, you'll still find that a photo is helpful for posing the figure and filling in the details. If you can't find a good photograph, combine the traits from two or three different

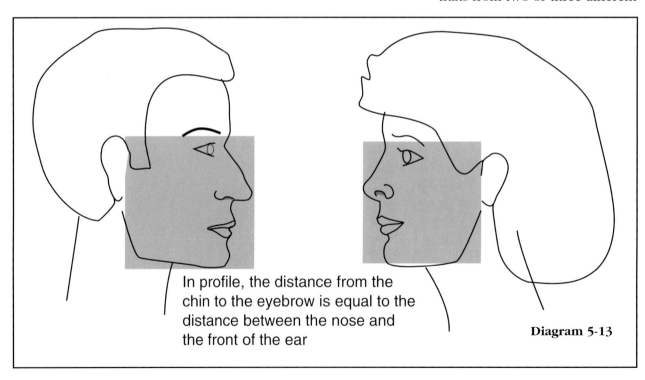

In profile, the distance from the chin to the eyebrow is equal to the distance between the nose and the front of the ear

Diagram 5-13

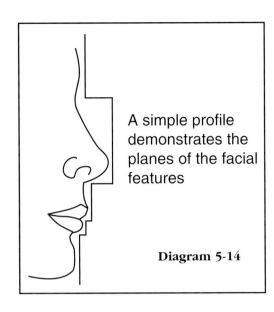

A simple profile demonstrates the planes of the facial features

Diagram 5-14

photographs to come up with the desired model. Don't forget that your best model is as close as your full-length mirror—just strike the pose you want to sculpt.

After you choose a model, study the main features of the face. Is the head round, oval, square, triangular, or heart-shaped? Is the nose narrow or wide? Is it rounded or sharp? Is it turned up at the end or straight? How prominent are the cheekbones? Are the cheeks hollow and sunken? Are the laugh lines barely visible or full and expressive? What about the shape of the eyes—are they almond, round, or teardrop-shaped? Are they wide-set, close together, bright, or sunken? Finally, are the lips wide or narrow, thick or thin?

These are just a few of the many variations that make a face unique. As you study faces you will notice many more differences, and you'll be able to capture those unique characteristics in clay.

ADDITIONAL READING

Faigin, Gary. *The Artist's Complete Guide to Facial Expressions* (New York: Watson-Guptill, 1990)

Hogarth, Burne. *Dynamic Figure Drawing* (New York: Watson-Guptill, 1970).

Peck, Stephen Rogers. *Atlas of Human Anatomy for the Artist* (New York: Oxford University Press, 1982).

Roche, Nan. *The New Clay: Techniques and Approaches to Jewelry Making* (Rockville, Md.: Flower Valley Press, 1991)

Sheppard, Joseph. *Realistic Figure Drawing* (Cincinnati, Ohio: North Light Books, 1991)

6
Make the Armature

The decision of which type of armature to use really depends on the desired pose of the figure. The flexible armature is easier to make because it is made from very thin wire; it's also easy to bend and shape. But once clay is added to the armature, the armature is not strong enough to hold a complicated pose. The reinforced armature is stronger and will hold its shape—even when used for a figure balanced on one leg—but the wire may break if it is bent too much before the clay is baked. The thin wire wrapped around the heavy wire on the reinforced armature provides a surface for the clay to grab.

For both types of armatures, use the appropriate template as a guide to ensure that the competed armature will be the appropriate size.

Flexible Armature

To shape the body, cut two lengths of 26-gauge wire according to the measurements listed with the template of your choice. For adult and teen figures, bend the longest piece of wire in half, then bend it in half again. Bend it in half a third time, this time holding your finger in the center section, as shown in Diagram 6-1. For young children and toddlers, bend the wire in half only twice, holding the center section after the first fold.

Twist the wires together down to the point where the wires separate to form the hips, then twist each leg separately. Use pliers to make sharp bends for the hips and feet (Diagram

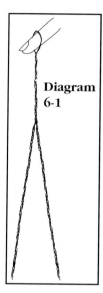

Diagram 6-1

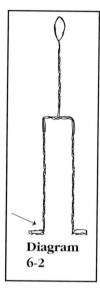

Diagram 6-2

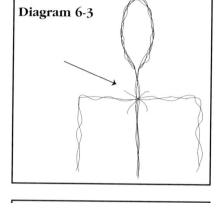

Diagram 6-3

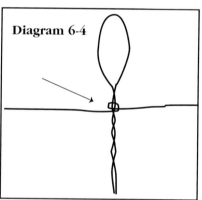

Diagram 6-4

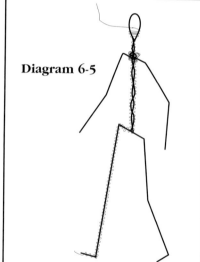

Diagram 6-5

6-2). Make the foot about ⅜" long and fold the wire back to meet the leg. Cut off excess length of wire.

To make the arms, fold the shorter wire in half, then fold it in half again. (For children and toddlers, fold the wire in half only once.) Attach the arms to the body by criss-crossing a short piece of wire around the body and arms four or five times as shown in Diagram 6-3. Give the wrap a squeeze with the pliers to cinch it tight. Bend at the shoulders.

6-1

6-2

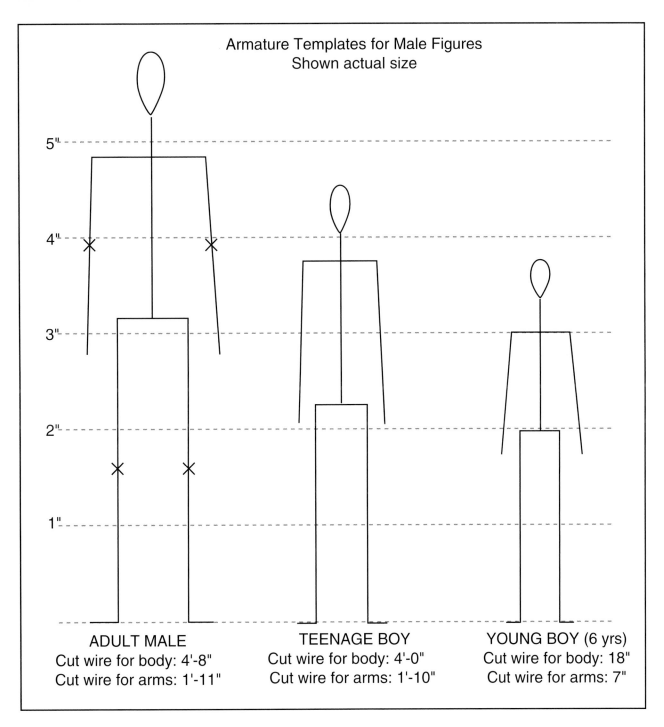

Armature Templates for Male Figures
Shown actual size

5"

4"

3"

2"

1"

ADULT MALE
Cut wire for body: 4'-8"
Cut wire for arms: 1'-11"

TEENAGE BOY
Cut wire for body: 4'-0"
Cut wire for arms: 1'-10"

YOUNG BOY (6 yrs)
Cut wire for body: 18"
Cut wire for arms: 7"

Bend the completed armature into the desired pose. You will be re-bending and refining the position of the armature as you work on the doll, but get it as close as possible to the desired position before adding any clay.

Reinforced Armature

The wire lengths provided are approximate, so compare your armature with the template as you work. Cut a length of 18-gauge wire according to the measurement listed with the template of your choice. Make a loop in the center of the wire for the head. Holding the head loop with the pliers, twist the wires together to form the torso. At the bottom of the torso, bend the wires away from each other to shape the hips, legs, and feet. Make the feet about 3⁄8″ long and fold back the excess wire, if any, to meet the legs. Cut off any excess wire.

Cut a 5″ length of 18-gauge wire for the arms. Bend the wire once around the body as shown in Diagram 6-4 and cinch tight with pliers. Check the armature with the template to make sure the arms are in the right place, then wrap a short piece of thin wire around the joint to help hold the arms in place. (This joint will be reinforced later.)

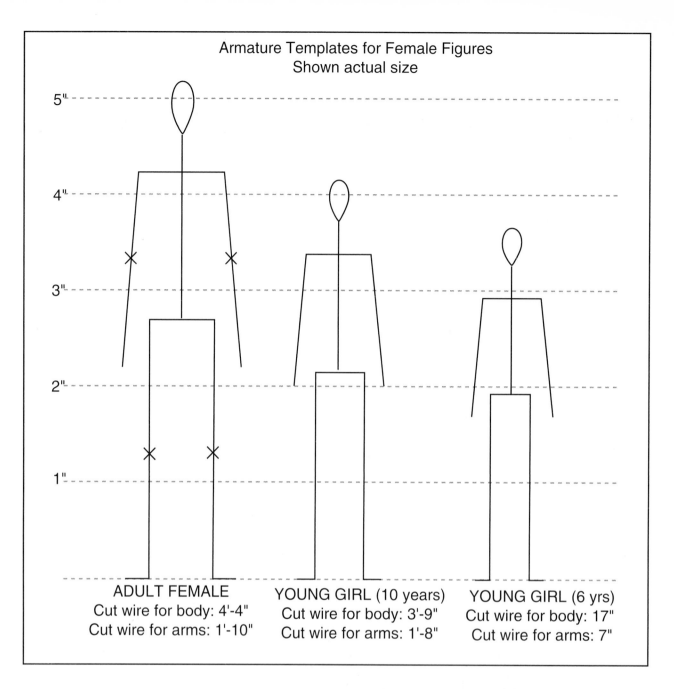

Armature Templates for Female Figures
Shown actual size

5"

4"

3"

2"

1"

ADULT FEMALE
Cut wire for body: 4'-4"
Cut wire for arms: 1'-10"

YOUNG GIRL (10 years)
Cut wire for body: 3'-9"
Cut wire for arms: 1'-8"

YOUNG GIRL (6 yrs)
Cut wire for body: 17"
Cut wire for arms: 7"

Bend the arm wires at the shoulders and cut the arms off at the length indicated on the armature template (Photo 6-1).

Cut a 4-foot length of 26-gauge wire and wrap the entire armature. Start wrapping at the end of one foot and work up the torso; criss-cross the joint of the arms and torso several times before continuing to the head as shown in Diagram 6-5 and Photo 6-2. Thread the wire through the head loop several times until the loop is completely filled. Wrap the wire back down the torso, ending at the second foot. Cut off excess wire. (If you run short of wire, add another piece.) Cut another piece of 26-gauge wire and wrap the arms, starting at the end of one arm, criss-crossing the joint again a few times, and finishing at the end of the second arm.

Carefully bend the armature into the desired position, using the X marks on the armature templates to place the bends for the elbows and knees. Keep the arms clear of the face at this point.

7
Sculpt a Solid-Body Figure

Photo by Alice Korach

Even if this is your first attempt at figure sculpting, you may choose to sculpt your own model. Simply follow the steps in the order presented but vary the pose, facial features, and other distinguishing details. The most important thing to remember is to enjoy the process of watching your figure take shape and become uniquely yours!

The process of sculpting the all-clay, solid-body figure is divided into four sections: cover the armature, build the figure, add the head and facial features, finish and refine the figure. Remember that the process of sculpting the figure takes time, so don't look for the finished figure during the early steps. Just keep working along and adding clay to your armature; by the time you reach the final steps your figure will emerge.

Because much of the pliability of the clay comes from the warmth of your hands, roll the balls of clay around in your hands a little before adding the pieces to the armature. The measurements referred to in the instructions are for an adult figure (male or female) and are intended to be general guidelines. Adjust the sizes of the clay pieces when working on smaller figures.

Cover the Armature
• **Photo 7-1:**

a) Make a reinforced armature for an adult female as shown in Chapter 6 and bend the armature into the desired position.

b) Roll two balls of clay, each ¾″ in diameter. Roll into cylinders

The step-by-step instructions that follow are for making an all-clay figure. You may, however, choose to start with the cloth-body figure demonstrated in Chapter 8. The techniques for sculpting the head, hands, and feet are essentially the same. Regardless of which type of figure you choose to make first, you may find it useful to scan the photos in both chapters.

Do not feel as if you have to make the exact figures demonstrated in these two chapters.

25

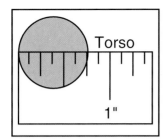

Torso

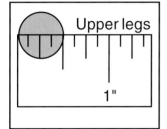

Upper legs

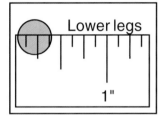

Lower legs

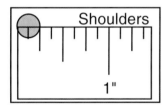

Shoulders

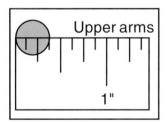

Upper arms

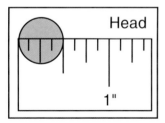

Head

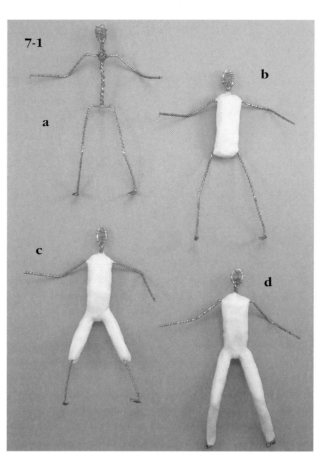

7-1

a b c d

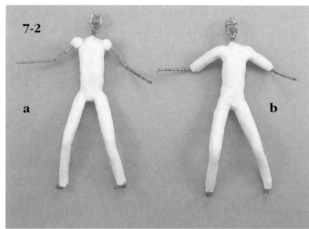

7-2

a b

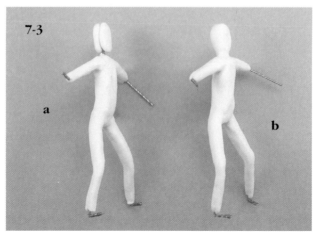

7-3

a b

as long as the torso. Flatten the cylinders slightly. Place on front and back of the torso. Sandwich and roll seams smooth, using the cuticle stick. Use a light touch—the clay should hold its shape overall.

c) For the right upper leg, roll two balls of clay, each ½″ in diameter. Roll into cylinders as long as the upper leg. Sandwich and roll smooth. Do the same for the left upper leg. Note: You're not forming a knee at this point, so just estimate the placement of the joint between the upper and lower leg. (It's easier to work the legs in two sections rather than in one long section.)

d) For the right lower leg, roll two balls of clay ⅜″ in diameter. Roll into cylinders as long as the lower leg. Sandwich and roll smooth. Do the same for the left lower leg.

• **Photo 7-2:**

a) For the right shoulder, sandwich shoulder wire between two ¼″ balls and roll smooth. Do the same for the left shoulder.

b) For the right upper arm, roll two ⅜″ balls. Shape into cylinders as long as the upper arm. Sandwich and roll smooth. Do the same for the left arm. Leave the lower arm uncovered for now.

• **Photo 7-3:**

a) For the head, roll two balls ½″ in diameter (remember to use the tinted clay, if applicable). Shape into ovals and flatten slightly. Each oval should be just large enough to cover the wire head. Sandwich the head wire between the flattened ovals.

b) Roll the seams on the head smooth. The head will look small—don't worry. When you add hair and facial structures later, it will be the right size. Roll some of the clay down to start the neck.

Leave the feet, lower arms, and hands uncovered for the time. The clay has a tendency to "drift" down as it's worked; with the feet and arm wires bare, you can grab the wires and push the clay back into place.

Build the Figure

Even though you will be sculpting clothes onto the figure, it's necessary to shape the clay body as if it will be nude. Later, when you add the clay clothes, they will fit and hang more naturally. Remember that the human figure is bilaterally symmetrical, so build evenly—whatever you do to one side, do the same to the other.

Check the position of your armature and make adjustments, if necessary. If you find the model's position makes working on the figure awkward, just get it as close as possible until the final stages. For example, if your figure's arms are folded in front, leave the arms sticking straight out until the torso is completed, then move the arms into position and finish them last.

As you work on the figure, the warmth of your hands may cause the clay to soften and shift. If the shoulders creep up, roll them back down into place. If the arms stretch, hold the bare wire and push the clay back up—same for the legs. Adjust for clay shift frequently. If the clay starts to get too pliable, let your work rest for an hour or so to cool and become firmer.

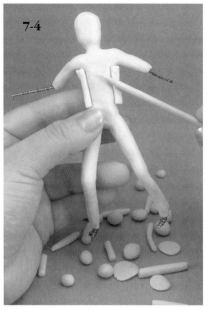

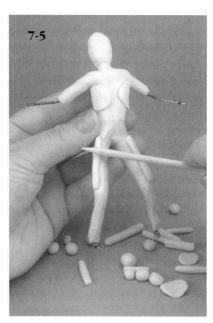

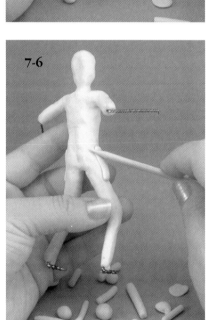

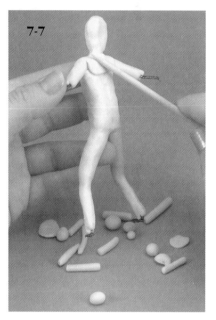

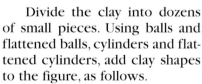

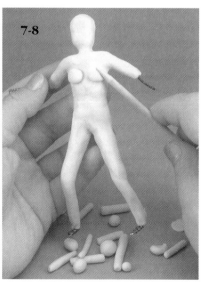

Divide the clay into dozens of small pieces. Using balls and flattened balls, cylinders and flattened cylinders, add clay shapes to the figure, as follows.
- **Photo 7-4:** Form two identically shaped cylinders and place one on each side of the torso. Roll smooth.
- **Photo 7-5:** Add flattened circles to build up the chest; add cylinders to build up the upper legs.
- **Photos 7-6, 7-7, 7-8, 7-9, 7-10 and 7-11:** Add pieces of clay and roll smooth to build up the thighs, shoulders, breasts,

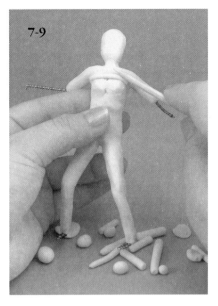

7-9

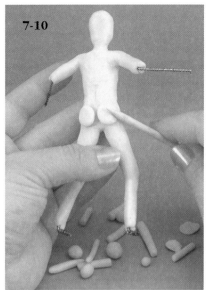

7-10

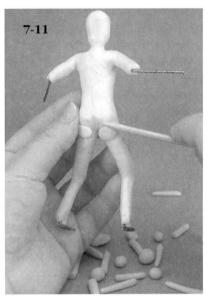

7-11

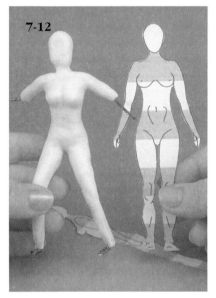

7-12

want flecks of dirt and dust to show up in your figure's face.

Although the steps for sculpting the face are presented in a linear manner, the process is more circular. Minor changes in one feature can affect other features, so work a little on each feature in turn, using a rotation system. Work on the nose, for example, then the lips, cheeks, and eyes (in whatever order is more natural for you). Check the shape of the head; check the profile of the face. Work on the nose a little more, then the lips, cheeks, and so on. Keep working around and around the face until the features start to work together and achieve a final appearance.

• **Photo 7-13:** To build up the back of the head, add two or

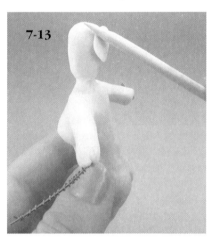

7-13

chest and buttocks, and legs as shown. Continue working around the figure in the same manner. Do not work on the head, feet, lower arms, or hands yet. As your figure starts to take shape, use smaller and smaller pieces of clay. If you find it necessary to scrape away clay, the pieces with which you are building are too large. To overcome the natural tendency to use pieces that are too large, select a piece that you think is about the right size, cut the piece in half, then cut them in half again to achieve a workable size.

• **Photo 7-12:** Compare your figure with "ideal" body illustra-

tions and with your own photos and sketches. Work on the rough figure until you achieve the general shape of the figure. Because you will be holding the figure extensively as you work on head and facial features, don't work on perfecting features such as knees and elbows yet. Such fine details are added at the final stage.

Add the Head and Facial Features

When working on parts of the face, take extra care that your work surface, hands, and tools are absolutely clean! You don't

three flattened balls, one at a time. Roll smooth after each. Build a bald head—hair is added later.

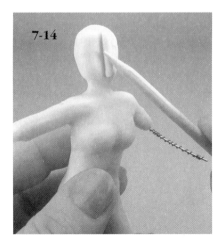

7-14

• **Photo 7-14:** Roll the front of the head smooth in preparation for the facial features. Add a small rope to the center of the face, vertically, and blend, creating a gentle roundness.

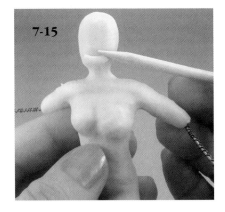

• **Photo 7-15:** Roll a ⅛″ ball of clay into a rope and add it to the chin line. Roll smooth, creating the beginnings of a chin.

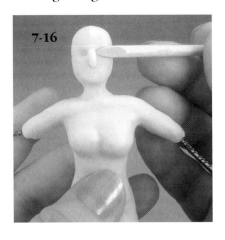

• **Photo 7-16:** Make a rope about one-third as long as the length of the face from the chin to the crown; place the rope in the center third of this section to establish the position of the nose. To place the eyes, use the rounded side of the cuticle stick to form a depression on each side of the nose. Place the eyes halfway between the chin and the top of the head. Feather the sides of the nose cylinder into the face. (At this point the face looks pretty funny—and in profile it looks even funnier. Don't worry—it will all come together!)

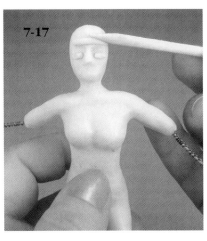

• **Photo 7-17:** Add a rope for the brow ridge and small cylinders for the cheekbones. Roll smooth. Continue to add tiny pieces of clay to the cheeks until the cheeks look about right.

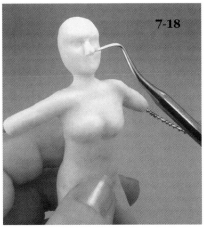

• **Photo 7-18:** Add a small ball of clay to the tip of the nose and roll smooth.

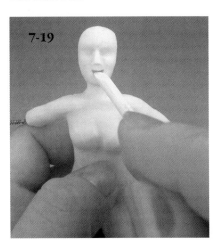

• **Photo 7-19:** Using the rounded end of the cuticle stick, gently press in to open the mouth. Shape the edges of the mouth to achieve the desired shape. (Both figures in this book show examples of sculpting an open mouth. If you choose to give your figure a closed mouth, use a fine, sharp edge to scribe the center line of the smile. Build up the lips in the same manner as for an open-mouth smile.)

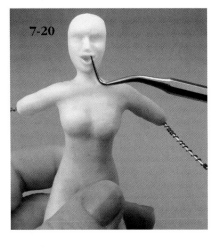

• **Photo 7-20:** Add very thin ropes of clay to build up the upper and lower lips.

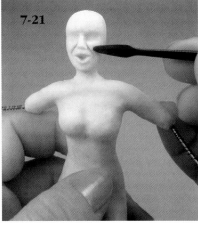

• **Photo 7-21:** Use the edge of the cuticle stick to define the "laugh lines." Add a thin rope of clay just above the laugh lines to emphasize cheeks and laugh lines.
• **Photo 7-22:** Flatten a very small ball of clay and place it in the mouth to form the tongue. Make a shallow depression down the center of the tongue.

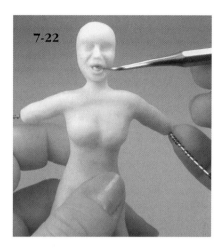

Define the edge between the tongue and the lips.

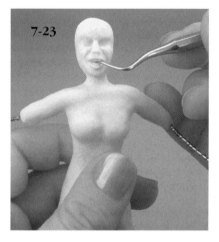

• **Photo 7-23:** Simulate the top row of teeth with a thin rope of clay. Set the teeth slightly back from the edge of the top lip and smooth the surface, making sure the teeth curve slightly.

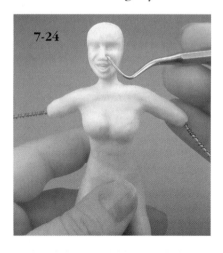

• **Photo 7-24:** Pull down some of the clay from the sides of the

nose to form the nostrils. (If the nose is already thin, make the nostrils by adding small balls of clay to the sides of the nose.)

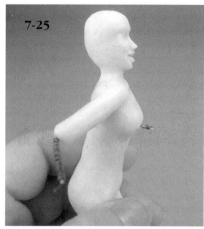

• **Photo 7-25:** Check the proportions of the face. If the cheeks "climb" up the sides of the nose, use the flat side of the cuticle stick to separate the cheeks from the nose. Make sure the cheeks wrap around the face and don't just sit under the eyes. Redefine the hollow area for the eyes. Check the face in profile.

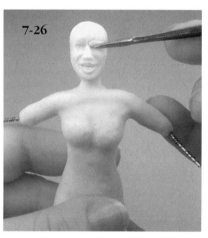

• **Photo 7-26:** The profile revealed that the eyes were a little higher than the halfway mark; ropes of clay added to the top of the eye hollow bring them back into place.
• **Photo 7-27:** Roll the eye areas smooth, then scribe lines to define the upper and lower eyelids.
• **Photo 7-28:** Add a small rope above each upper eyelid

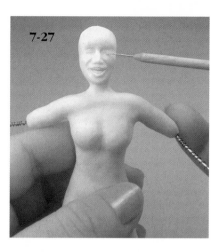

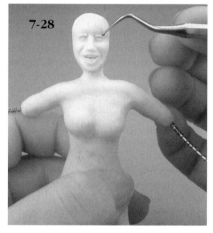

up the brow ridge. Add very thin ropes of clay just above the scribed line for the upper eyelid. Smooth the surface of the eyes to establish the shape and round the eyes slightly. Make sure the eyes match; test the evenness of the eyes by looking at the figure upside down.
• **Photo 7-29:** Compare the profile of the face again and make adjustments, if necessary. (A little

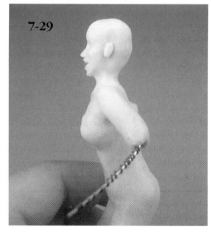

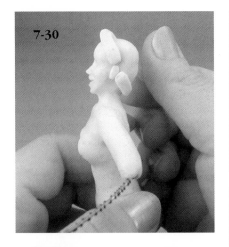

7-30

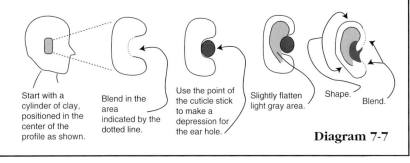

Start with a cylinder of clay, positioned in the center of the profile as shown.

Blend in the area indicated by the dotted line.

Use the point of the cuticle stick to make a depression for the ear hole.

Slightly flatten light gray area.

Shape.

Blend.

Diagram 7-7

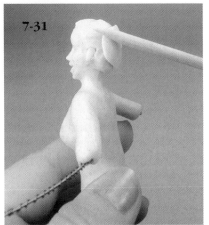

7-31

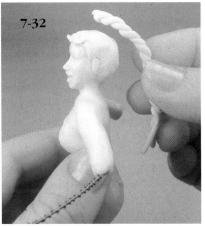
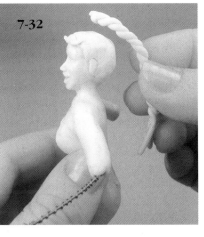

7-32

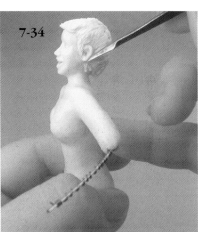

7-34

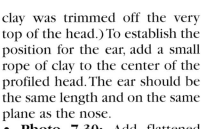
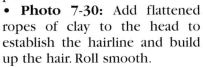

7-33

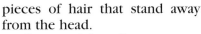

7-35

clay was trimmed off the very top of the head.) To establish the position for the ear, add a small rope of clay to the center of the profiled head. The ear should be the same length and on the same plane as the nose.

- **Photo 7-30:** Add flattened ropes of clay to the head to establish the hairline and build up the hair. Roll smooth.

- **Photo 7-31:** Fill in the hair with more flattened circles. Feather the edges of the clay where it forms the hairline.

- **Photo 7-32:** To make a French-braid hair style as shown, braid three thin ropes of clay and cut the piece to fit along the back of the head. Make a depression along the center part of the hair on the head. Press the braid into place.

- **Photo 7-33:** Finish shaping the hair, then use a fine-edge tool to scribe lines to indicate hair. Be sure to add bangs and other

pieces of hair that stand away from the head.

- **Photo 7-34:** Follow Diagram 7-7 to shape the ear.

Refine the Figure

The following steps demonstrate how to add clay clothes to the figure. You may also choose to leave the clay figure nude and glue on fabric clothes after the figure is baked.

- **Photo 7-35:** When you are satisfied with the face and hair, turn your attention back to the body.

Refine the shapes of the torso, arms, and legs. Build up the clay to make the boots, or follow Diagram 7-8 to make bare feet.

- **Photo 7-36:** Wrap flattened ropes of clay around the legs to establish the positions of the waistline and legs of the shorts. Fill in with more flattened pieces of clay.

- **Photo 7-37:** Add another flattened rope to make the neckline of the shirt. Make the folds in the waistline of the shorts by

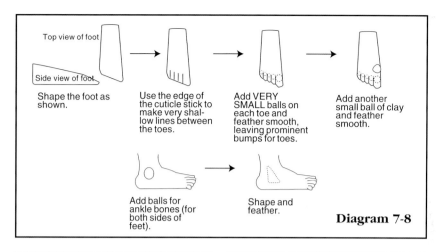

Top view of foot

Side view of foot

Shape the foot as shown.

Use the edge of the cuticle stick to make very shallow lines between the toes.

Add VERY SMALL balls on each toe and feather smooth, leaving prominent bumps for toes.

Add another small ball of clay and feather smooth.

Add balls for ankle bones (for both sides of feet).

Shape and feather.

Diagram 7-8

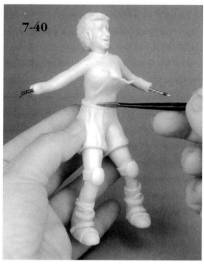

7-40

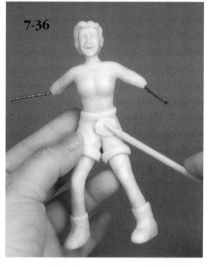

7-36

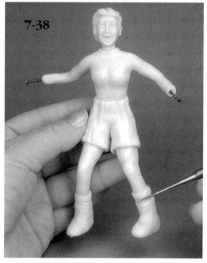

7-38

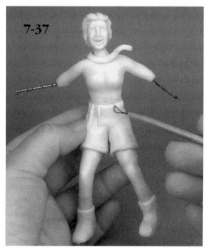

7-37

7-39

7-41

- **Photo 7-40:** To make each knee protector, flatten a small ball of clay and cup slightly. Place over the band on top of the knee. Cut a rectangle of clay and arrange to form the bib of the overalls. Add defining elastic lines to the waistband of the overalls.

- **Photo 7-41:** Add a belt, fanny pack, and overall straps. Cut off about ½″ from the ends of the arm wires, leaving just enough to grab hold of the clay for the

removing slivers of clay with the scooping wire and adding tapered ropes.

- **Photo 7-38:** Add clay for the forearms, leaving about ⅝″ of the end of the wire bare. Add flattened ropes for socks. Press grooves into the socks to simulate folds.

- **Photo 7-39:** Roll out a thin piece of clay. Add narrow strips of clay to the boots to simulate bootstraps. Roll the textured end of the X-Acto knife or similar tool over the clay to add texture. Wrap a band of textured clay around each knee to simulate bands holding the knee protectors.

hands (⅛″ or so). Make the hands separately, using the patterns and instructions in Diagrams 7-9 through 7-12 and choosing hands with articulated fingers (each finger is separate), "mitten" hands (all four fingers

Men and Teen Boys

Women and Teen Girls

Children

Include gray area for hands on cloth-body figures;
use white part of patterns for all-clay figures

Diagram 7-9

7-42

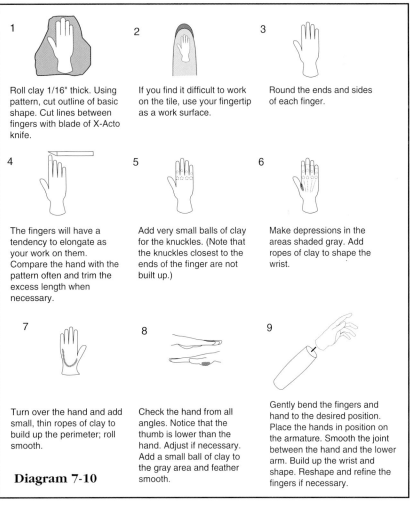

1 Roll clay 1/16" thick. Using pattern, cut outline of basic shape. Cut lines between fingers with blade of X-Acto knife.

2 If you find it difficult to work on the tile, use your fingertip as a work surface.

3 Round the ends and sides of each finger.

4 The fingers will have a tendency to elongate as your work on them. Compare the hand with the pattern often and trim the excess length when necessary.

5 Add very small balls of clay for the knuckles. (Note that the knuckles closest to the ends of the finger are not built up.)

6 Make depressions in the areas shaded gray. Add ropes of clay to shape the wrist.

7 Turn over the hand and add small, thin ropes of clay to build up the perimeter; roll smooth.

8 Check the hand from all angles. Notice that the thumb is lower than the hand. Adjust if necessary. Add a small ball of clay to the gray area and feather smooth.

9 Gently bend the fingers and hand to the desired position. Place the hands in position on the armature. Smooth the joint between the hand and the lower arm. Build up the wrist and shape. Reshape and refine the fingers if necessary.

Diagram 7-10

are together), or closed hands. Do as much work on the hands as possible before adding them to the figure.

• **Photo 7-42:** Set the figure on the tile. Using spare pieces of clay, make props to ensure that the figure will remain in position during baking. Make the props thick enough to support the figure, but position the props in such as way that there is minimal contact with the figure.

Look over the figure and consider adding some finishing touches.

• To add movement to the clothes use a rounded tool to gently stretch and lift the edges of the clay fabric.

• To add dimensional details such as pockets, collars, ribbons, bows, flowing sleeves, and ties,

roll out the clay to the desired thickness, cut out the piece, shape as desired, and attach to the figure.

• To add texture, press items such as Styrofoam, leather tools, various types of fabric, sandpaper, and toothbrush bristles into the clay.

When you are satisfied with the figure, dip a small, flat sable paintbrush in denatured alcohol, then blot the brush on a paper towel. What remains on the brush is enough to use for smoothing the clay. Brush over the face very lightly. The denatured alcohol is used just to

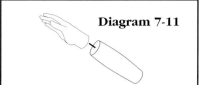

Diagram 7-11

Follow the steps for articulated fingers, but instead of cutting the lines between the fingers as shown in Step 1, use the edge of the cuticle stick to slightly score the finger lines. Continue through the steps. At Step 9, select a simple pose for the hands such as the one shown.

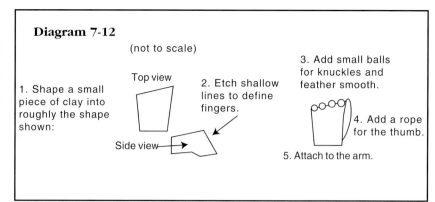

Diagram 7-12

(not to scale)

1. Shape a small piece of clay into roughly the shape shown:

Top view

Side view

2. Etch shallow lines to define fingers.

3. Add small balls for knuckles and feather smooth.

4. Add a rope for the thumb.

5. Attach to the arm.

7-43

Photo by Alice Korach

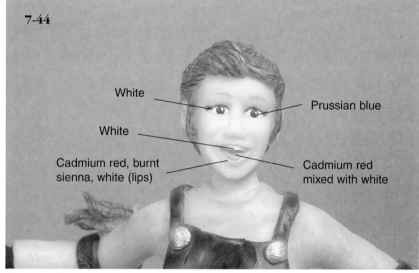

7-44

White

White

Prussian blue

Cadmium red, burnt sienna, white (lips)

Cadmium red mixed with white

Photo by Alice Korach

smooth out any sharp edges, not to shape the clay. Use it sparingly—too much may weaken the clay. Let the denatured alcohol dry for at least an hour before baking.

Test the oven temperature and bake according to the guidelines in Chapter 2. Allow the figure to cool in the oven completely before moving.

• **Photo 7-43:** Back view of the finished figure. Paint the figure as desired, or use the following colors to paint the figure as shown. (All colors are Schmincke Aero Colors unless noted.)

Overalls: Three parts rose madder (no. 344) mixed with one part sapphire blue (no. 440) Shirt: Indian yellow (no. 230)

Tights: one part rose madder (no. 344) mixed with four parts line white (no. 110)

Knee/elbow pads: green (no. 540)

Hair: umber (no. 620)

Boots: purple glitter nail polish over Apple Barrel True Navy

Buttons: Accent Crown Jewels gold

Socks: Ceramcoat yellow

• **Photo 7-44:** Paint the eyes and lips as shown. Oil paints

were used for the sample, but you may use acrylic paints, if you wish.

Allow the paint several days to cure, then document your remarkable efforts by signing your one-of-a-kind figure with a fine-line black permanent felt pen.

Now that you've learned the basics of figure sculpting, just follow the same techniques to make any type of figure you like—all you need is imagination! The next chapter will show you one variation on these techniques—making a figure with a cloth body.

8
Sculpt a Cloth-Body Doll

The silver-clad, cloth-body doll has fabric clothes; the clay body and clothes for the gold doll are made following the techniques in Chapter 7. All photos this chapter are by Alice Korach.

The techniques for sculpting the head, hands, and feet for the cloth-body figure are the same as those in Chapter 7. The cloth-body doll is a good choice if your want your figure to have a little flexibility and if you want it to have cloth clothes. The closed eyes and open mouth in the face of the rock star can be adapted to create a variety of expressions in many types of faces.

• **Photo 8-1:** Make a reinforced armature for an adult male and shape as shown.

• **Photo 8-2:** Roll two ⅝″ balls of clay into cylinders; place one on each side of the arm-shoulder area. Squeeze to attach firmly. Gently roll the cuticle stick back and forth over the clay to smooth the seam and join the pieces.

• **Photo 8-3:** Roll two ½″ balls of clay and flatten slightly. Attach

8-1

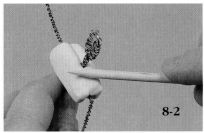

8-2

8-3

35

8-4

to each side of the head and roll smooth.

• **Photo 8-4:** To build the shape for the neck and back of the head, add very small pieces of clay and roll smooth. Notice that the face area is left flat.

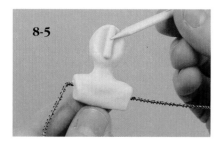

8-5

• **Photo 8-5:** Add a small rope to the face and blend, creating a gentle roundness.

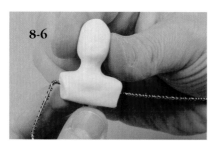

8-6

• **Photo 8-6:** Gently squeeze the sides of the head as needed to maintain the proper shape.

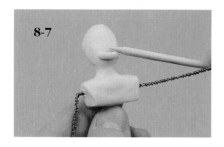

8-7

• **Photo 8-7:** Add a small rope to the chin and roll smooth. Add a small rope to establish the position of the nose.
• **Photo 8-8:** Define the eye area

8-8

by gently pushing in the clay with the back (rounded side) of the cuticle stick.

8-9

• **Photo 8-9:** Add a long rope for the brow and small ropes for the cheek bones; roll smooth. Blend the nose into the sides of the face and eye areas. Flatten the bridge of the nose.

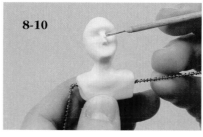

8-10

• **Photo 8-10:** Add a small ball for the tip of the nose and roll smooth. (The tool shown is from Perfect Touch.)

8-11

• **Photo 8-11:** Using a tool with a curved side, gently press in to open the mouth. Note that no clay is removed.
• **Photo 8-12:** Add small ropes

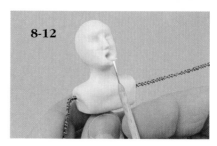

8-12

for upper and lower lips; blend smooth.

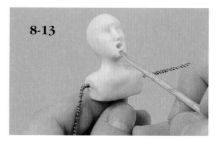

8-13

• **Photo 8-13:** Define the lower lip and chin by gently pushing in with the curved tool.

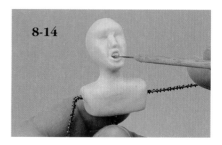

8-14

• **Photo 8-14:** Add preliminary "laugh lines." Add small ball of clay to the top of the mouth for the teeth. Gently shape the teeth to follow the curve of the mouth.

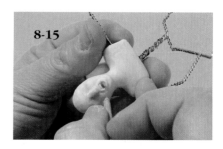

8-15

• **Photo 8-15:** Add a small flattened ball of clay for a tongue. Define the area between the tongue and lips.
• **Photo 8-16:** Trim excess clay to define the area under the nose.
• **Photo 8-17:** Now add more

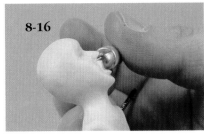
8-16

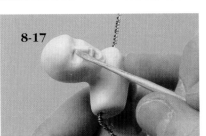
8-17

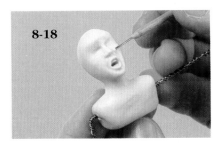
8-18

clay to build up the cheekbones.
• **Photo 8-18:** Add small balls of clay for the nostrils.

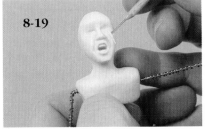
8-19

• **Photo 8-19:** Add small ropes of clay to build up the laugh lines, which start just above the nostrils. Smooth all face surfaces.

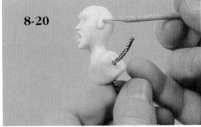
8-20

• **Photo 8-20:** Add small ropes to define the ear area. The ears should be centered in the pro-

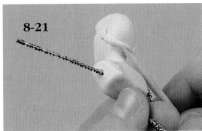
8-21

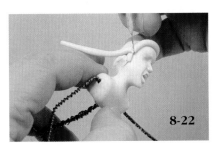
8-22

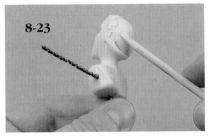
8-23

file and on the same plane as the nose.
• **Photos 8-21, 8-22, 8-23:** Add long, thin ropes of clay to define the hairline; roll smooth.

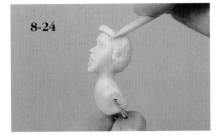
8-24

• **Photo 8-24:** Fill in the hair with thin, flattened pieces of clay. Continue to work on the hair until the profile of the head takes shape.

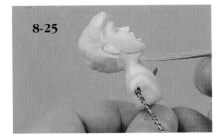
8-25

• **Photo 8-25:** Define the jaw line, which should end just below the earlobe.

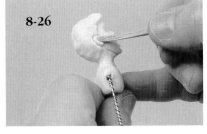
8-26

• **Photo 8-26:** Define the out-line of the ear. Press in on the inside of the ear. Then move the tool lower and press in again. Refer to the diagrams in Chapter 7 to add the finishing details to the ears.

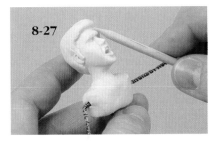
8-27

• **Photo 8-27:** Add ropes for sideburns; add small ropes to build up the forehead.

8-28

• **Photo 8-28:** Add small ropes to build up the eyes.

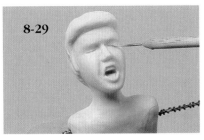
8-29

• **Photo 8-29:** Scribe a line to define the edge of the eyelids.

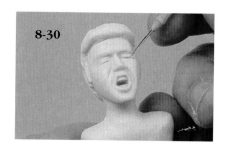

8-30

• **Photo 8-30:** Add a small rope above the scribed line to build up the eyelid.

8-31

• **Photo 8-31:** Define the gap between the eyebrows. This slope should extend gently from the bridge of the nose.

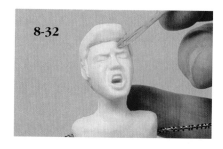

8-32

• **Photo 8-32:** Push down on the clay to define the curve of the eyebrows.

8-33

• **Photo 8-33:** Define the hair. The rounded tool shown is part of a four-part set from Squadron Products and is useful for making wavy hair. You can also define the hair by gently dragging the back of the X-Acto knife blade along the clay. Don't forget

to add details to the sideburns and eyebrows. Refine the shoulders and trim away excess clay, if necessary.

Finally, smooth all the surfaces with denatured alcohol applied sparingly with the sable paintbrush. This step helps create a translucent, skinlike effect; the skin areas will not be painted with anything else. Denatured alcohol is a solvent for polymer clay, so practice on the head and shoulder area and use a light touch.

(You can bake the head at this point, if desired, then come back and add the feet and bake the entire figure again.)

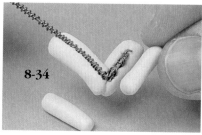

8-34

• **Photo 8-34:** Adjust the armature to the finished position. Add cylinders of clay to cover the feet; roll smooth. If your figure will be wearing shoes, build up the feet just enough to achieve the general shape shown in the diagrams in Chapter 7. After the figure is baked, you can trim away clay as needed to make the feet fit the shoes.
• **Photo 8-35:** Support the figure on a spare cylinder of clay, place on a ceramic tile, and bake

according to baking instructions in Chapter 2. Hot clay is very fragile, so do not move the piece until it has cooled completely.

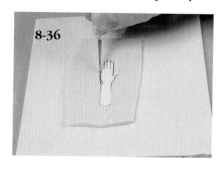

8-36

• **Photo 8-36:** Now roll out a 3/16″-thick sheet of clay and cut out the hands, using the patterns for adult male hands in Chapter 7.

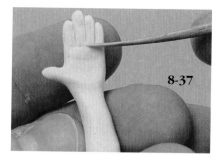

8-37

• **Photo 8-37:** Add clay to build up and round the forearm of the left (open) hand. Add ropes to define the palm of the hand; scribe in the finger lines and round the edges.
• **Photo 8-38:** Define the fingers on the back of the hand. Add small balls for knuckles; press in with a rounded tool to define the fingernails. Build up and shape the thumb.

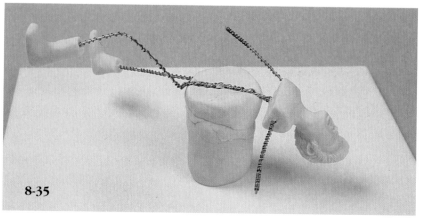

8-35

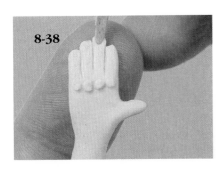

8-38

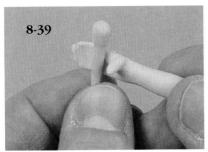

8-39

• **Photo 8-39:** Make a microphone as shown, bake and cool. Wrap the right hand around the microphone.

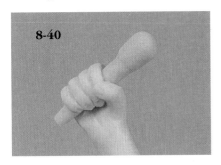

8-40

• **Photo 8-40:** Add details in the same manner as previously described.

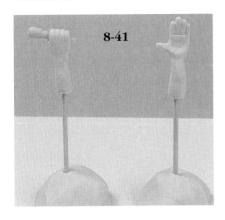

8-41

• **Photo 8-41:** Gently press about ½″ of a rounded toothpick into each arm. Stand the arms in spare clay on a ceramic tile and bake.

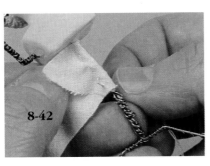

8-42

• **Photo 8-42:** The ends of the arm wires should be 2″ from the center of the chest. Measure and cut as needed. Build up the body with bias strips of muslin. Start the first strip by stitching the end.

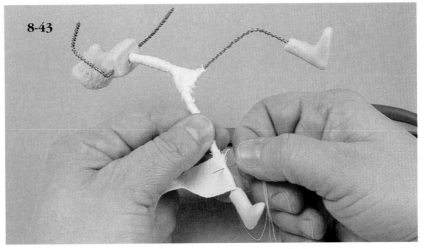

8-43

• **Photo 8-43:** Continue to wrap the body, ending and beginning each strip with a few stitches. Add small pieces of cotton batting to build out the sides of the torso (otherwise it will be round). Leave the figure lean until the clothes are made; you can always go back and add more padding as needed.

• **Photo 8-44:** Paint the lips, teeth, and tongue with the round brush and the hair with the flat brush; do not paint the skin. The sample uses bottle acrylic paints. When hair is dry, add that "greased-back" look by brushing the high spots with gloss medium.

• **Photo 8-45:** After all your work, your doll is ready for a flashy costume of your choice. Make your own costume, or

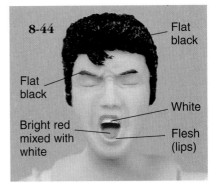

8-44

Flat black

Flat black

White

Bright red mixed with white

Flesh (lips)

follow the patterns for the beaded lamé outfit shown, which appeared in the August 1997 issue of *Nutshell News*. Wait until after the doll is dressed to

8-45

glue the arms onto the arm wires.

Congratulate yourself for sculpting a truly unique figure—and don't forget to sign your name to your work of art!

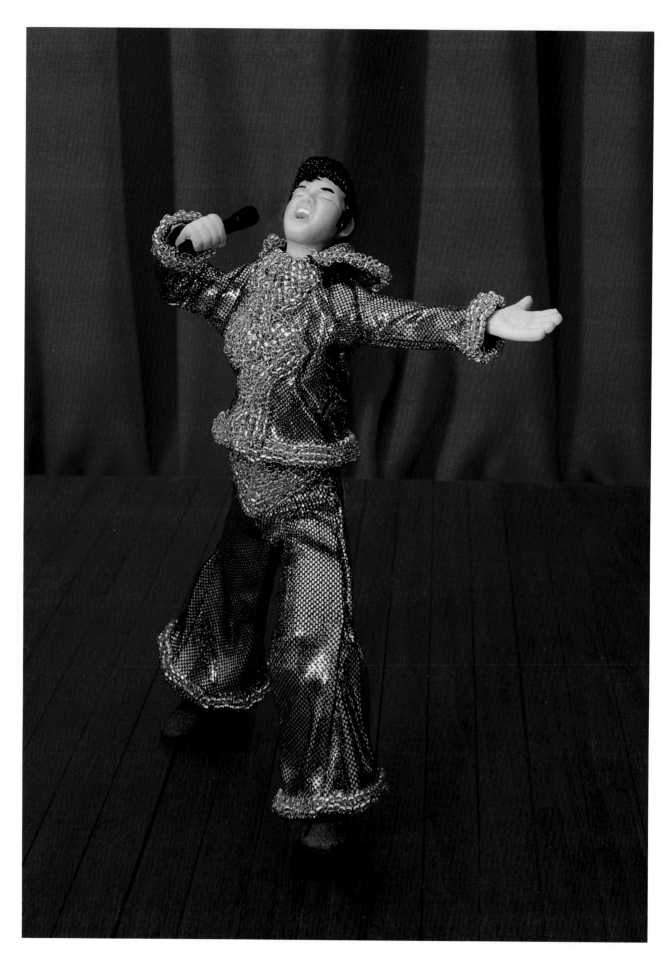

Color Gallery

"Calvin," who is painted with acrylic paints, is pondering what to do with the bugs now that he's found them. I used a drop of white glue to adhere the glass jar to the hand before adding the finishing details, and then baked the figure with the jar in hand. Notice how lifting up the clay in the lab coat and tie adds the idea of motion.

"Becky's" ponytail was made separately and added just before the figure was baked. The rounded back and joints help to convey the figure's emotions; the eyes are slightly exaggerated for comic effect. I painted the figure with acrylic paint and used glitter paint to add details to the tree and hair bow.

The fuzzy bunny slippers on "Bathtub Bob" and "Onslo" and the headband on "Becky" were covered with snow-texture medium. All three figures were painted with acrylic paint. Onslo was sculpted right in his easy chair, which was made from scrap pieces of clay. I used the textured sections of an X-Acto knife handle and a leather-working tool to add details to the bottom of Becky's shoes and Onslo's watch and T-shirt.

Fantasy figures provide opportunities to experiment with different types of mediums and textures. The robe on "Isis" was made by rolling a sheet of Delta Renaissance foil and copper-colored Sculpey III through a pasta machine. I painted "Helena's" sword and gold accessories with a mixture of powdered gold and high-gloss acrylic varnish. "Crystal's" cascading hair is painted with gold acrylic paint. "Harry" is a cloth-body figure whose fabric clothes are accented with accessories made from very thin leather. His knives are action-figure accessories that I improved with paint and jewels.

The fatigue of a hard day's work in a turn-of-the-century kitchen shows in "Grace's" slumped shoulders, puffed-out cheeks, and stringy hair. The skirt and apron were cut from thin sheets of clay and added to the body. After positioning her left hand, I added rolls of clay to the skirt under the hand to make it appear to be holding skirt folds.

Anatomical believability is just one of the two challenges offered by nude fantasy figures such as "Europa"; the other challenge is keeping the clay perfectly clean through the entire process. The lapis lazuli world that Europa "plays with as a ball" is more than ornamental—it counterbalances the weight of the hair. The silver accessories were painted with a mixture of powdered silver and high-gloss acrylic varnish.

"Catherine" (with pipe), "Linda" (sitting), and "Abigail" are from a series of western women figures. The skirts on Linda and Abigail are solid clay—the figures don't have legs. Catherine's skirt was rolled from thin clay, textured with a piece of heavy canvas, and added to the figure. All three were painted with acrylic paint; Linda's skin is painted with Pactra acrylic enamel, flat light earth, a very thin opaque paint that covers without leaving brush strokes or hiding details.

Just the fellas: "Ephrom," "Jamey," and "Adam." A beard can add a lot of personality to a male figure—and is much easier to sculpt than lips. The leather look of Jamey's vest, belt, and shoes is achieved with black Schmincke Aero Color. I textured the socks with the X-Acto knife handle and simulated the tartan pattern with thin brushstrokes of color.